ENERGY
Now and in the Future

Biomass Power

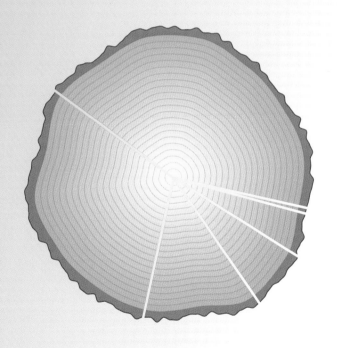

Neil Morris

A+
Smart Apple Media

Smart Apple Media
P.O. Box 3263
Mankato, MN 56002

Printed in the United States of America

Library of Congress Cataloging-in-Publication Data

Morris, Neil, 1946-
 Biomass power / by Neil Morris.
    p. cm. -- (Energy now and in the future)
 Includes index.
 ISBN 978-1-59920-337-9 (hardcover)
 1. Biomass energy--Juvenile literature. I. Title.
 TP339.M67 2010
 333.95'39--dc22

                                                                    2008053330

Designed by Helen James
Edited by Mary-Jane Wilkins
Artwork by Guy Callaby
Picture research by Su Alexander

Photograph acknowledgements
page 7 Martin Harvey; Gallo Images/Corbis; 9 Xavier Bertral/epa/Corbis;
11 Peter Johnson/Corbis; 12 Bettmann/Corbis; 14 Philippe Lissac/Godong/Corbis;
16 John Van Hasselt/Corbis; 18 Tim Graham/Alamy; 19 Kai Foersterling/epa/
Corbis; 20 Antoine Gyori/AGP/Corbis; 23 Sally A Morgan; Ecoscene/Corbis;
24 David Sailors/Corbis; 27 Bildagentur-online/Alamy; 28 Lasse Hejdenberg/
Hejlosa Bilder Ltd; 31 Everett Kennedy Brown/epa/Corbis; 32 Stan Pritchard/
Alamy; 35 Car Culture/Corbis; 36 Andrew Brookes/Corbis; 37 Paul A Souders/
Corbis; 38 Paulo Fridman/Corbis; 39 China Daily/Reuters/Corbis; 40 Andrew Fox/
Alamy; 42 Zhang Chuanqi/Xinhua Press/Corbis
Front cover Zhang Chuanqi/Xinhua Press/Corbis

9 8 7 6 5 4 3 2 1

Contents

The World of Living Things

Scientists call all organic matter (or living things) biomass. The term comes from the Greek word *bios* (meaning life) and mass (meaning quantity of matter). Today, we also use the term biomass to mean organic matter that can be used as a source of fuel or energy.

For thousands of years, people have burned wood and other plants as fuels to provide heat for warmth and cooking. In more recent times, we have found ways to use biomass as an energy source to power machines and produce electricity.

Passing on Solar Energy

All the world's energy originally comes from our nearest star, the Sun. This means that solar power is the ultimate energy source. All forms of biomass—plants and animals—are totally dependent on the Sun's electromagnetic radiation, which is a range of electrical and magnetic waves of energy. These are sent to Earth in the form of heat and light.

Plants change the Sun's energy waves (which we often call sunbeams) into chemical energy, which they can store and use to live. In this way, the world's biomass acts as a store of solar energy, which is very useful for both animals and humans.

Producing Food

Plants use energy from sunlight to combine carbon dioxide and water to make their own sugary food. A green pigment in plants' leaves, called chlorophyll, takes in the light. The pigment uses the light to make a simple form of sugar using water from the soil (drawn up through the plant's roots) combined with carbon dioxide (taken in from the air).

In this community of living things in Africa, a primary consumer reaches high to feed on a producer. The consumer is an elephant, and the tree's leaves produce the food.

This process is called photosynthesis, from Greek words meaning "putting together with light." During the process, plants give off oxygen, which all other living things (including humans) need to breathe and stay alive.

Supporting Ecosystems

The plants and animals that make up our planet's biomass live in many different habitats around the world. Groups of living things interact with each other and form communities. Every community and its environment of nonliving things, such as rocks, soil, and water, form an ecosystem.

All living things depend on food for energy. Scientists call plants producers because they produce food. Animals are called consumers because they eat plants for food. Primary consumers, such as rabbits and elephants, eat plants to get the energy they need to live and survive. Meat-eating animals, such as foxes and lions, are called secondary consumers because they gain energy by eating other animals.

Renewable Resource

Biomass is called a renewable resource because it can be replaced and should never run out. Other energy sources—such as coal, oil, and natural gas—are burned and used up to produce power. These are called nonrenewable because their stocks are used up and it takes millions of years for them to form underground. However, the world's plants grow very quickly, which is why they are classified as renewable, along with geothermal, solar, water, and wind power.

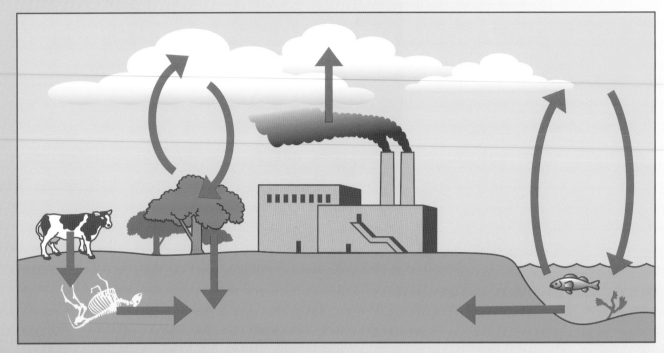

Carbon Cycle

Biomass forms part of the carbon cycle. During the process of photosynthesis, plants take carbon from the atmosphere in the form of carbon dioxide (CO_2). Plants also give out a small amount of CO_2. Animals take in carbon when they eat plants or other animals. When animals breathe out, they give off CO_2. Their waste also contains carbon, and this is digested by microscopic organisms, such as microbes, called decomposers. The decomposers also give off CO_2. When animals die, their remains are eaten by other scavenger animals or by tiny decomposers. Both give off

This illustration shows how carbon moves around Earth's ecosystems, including its oceans. Biomass plays a vital role in the natural cycle. Factories also release carbon dioxide from fossil fuels into the atmosphere. This increases the greenhouse effect (see below).

The Greenhouse Effect and Global Warming

Earth's atmosphere prevents some of the Sun's rays from reaching Earth. Its gases also stop some heat escaping from Earth, just as glass traps warmth inside a greenhouse. We are adding to this natural greenhouse effect by emitting so many waste gases from power plants, factories, and cars. Some of these greenhouse gases—especially carbon dioxide—are produced when we burn biomass to release energy. Experts have discovered that, in this way, humans are making natural climate change more extreme. Much of our energy use is adding to global warming, and land, sea, and air temperatures are gradually increasing. Using renewable energy sources can help to reduce the increase in global warming.

Why Is Biomass Carbon Neutral?

When we use biomass as a fuel and burn it, carbon goes back into the atmosphere as carbon dioxide. This speeds up a natural process that occurs when plants or animals die. If we make sure that the biomass harvested and used is replaced by newly planted material (which will take in CO_2), the fuel use is considered to be carbon neutral. It is called neutral because using (or burning) it does not add to the amount of carbon circulating in the natural cycle, but it does not remove carbon either. The environmental group Greenpeace International says: "When biomass is used to generate energy in an efficient and sustainable way, it has a role to play in reducing greenhouse gas (GHG) emissions and we strongly support this." Nevertheless, burning biomass does give off CO_2. This is why many environmentalists do not believe that it is as good as other renewable energy sources.

CO_2. In this way, carbon moves through ecosystems, as well as to and from Earth's atmosphere. This movement is called the carbon cycle, and it helps to keep a natural balance of carbon dioxide and oxygen.

Biomass versus Fossil Fuels

The world's main fossil fuels are coal, oil, and natural gas. These are called fossil fuels because they were formed from the fossilized remains of prehistoric organic matter— either plants or animals. In other words, these fuels were formed by the remains of prehistoric biomass and stored carbon underground. Scientists consider fossil fuels to be outside the natural carbon cycle and they are nonrenewable, unlike biomass (see page 7).

This dry riverbed in northeastern Spain shows the effects of drought in 2008. Experts believe that global warming is increasing drought conditions around the world.

Ancient and Modern Fires

Archaeologists and historians believe that wood was the first fuel used by humans. Ever since people learned to kindle and control fire many hundreds of thousands of years ago, it has been a vital source of heat, light, and power. In many parts of the world, and for many people, collecting firewood is still one of the most important tasks of the day.

Mastering Fire

We cannot know for certain when humans first mastered fire. Some experts believe that prehistoric people first had to conquer a natural fear of fire, which they shared with all animals. The first users of fire were probably men and women of the early human species called *Homo ergaster* (meaning workman because they developed many tools) or the related *Homo erectus* (upright man). The oldest evidence of fire use is found in patches of baked earth in Kenya, East Africa, which are more than 1.4 million years old. A cave site near Beijing, China, shows evidence of the remains of cooked meals from about 500,000 years ago.

Traditional Biomass

Today, energy experts refer to firewood (or fuelwood) as traditional biomass. Burning leaves, charcoal (see page 13), rice husks, and farming waste is considered traditional. Converting biomass into advanced biofuels (see page 16), such as gas and electricity, is called modern biomass energy use. Experts estimate that 10 percent of world energy used for cooking and heating comes from traditional biomass and supplies more than one-third of the world's people. In Africa, nearly three-quarters of the population rely on firewood. Many people in developing countries have no choice about the fuel they use—they can collect wood for free and could not afford alternatives even if they were available. In rich, industrialized parts of the world, traditional biomass is used much less as an energy source.

Kindling and Using Fire

Early people may have learned how fires started when they saw a forest fire caused by a lightning strike. They might have tried producing sparks by striking rocks together or rubbing sticks. Some must have succeeded in deliberately setting wood alight and controlling their own fire. This brought them great benefits. Fire provided warmth and could light the depths of a cave. It also offered protection from wild animals, which were as frightened of fire as humans had once been. Perhaps most importantly, fire could cook meat, which made it much easier and safer to eat. Cooked meat was more digestible, and the heat killed microorganisms that might otherwise have made people ill.

These people in Botswana are starting a fire by rubbing sticks together.

Fire as a Focus

Experts believe that from about 130,000 years ago, or perhaps earlier, groups of people started building hearths, or fireplaces. These became an important feature of prehistoric shelters. People came together to cook and eat, which must have made them feel closer to each other and strengthened family and group ties. They also learned to heat stones in the fireplace and drop them into a skin-lined pit of water to heat it. They could use the hot water for cooking and washing.

Prometheus and Vesta

Fire was seen as a vital, powerful force in ancient Greece and Rome. Greek myths tell the story of Prometheus, one of the family of giant gods called Titans. When the king of the gods, Zeus, was angry and decided not to allow humans fire, Prometheus stole a spark from heaven and gave fire back to the world. In Roman religion, Vesta was the goddess of the hearth who was worshipped in every Roman household. A sacred fire was kept in her honor at a small round temple in the Roman Forum.

Producing Goods

In ancient times, people used wood-burning fires to heat clay and metals. People in Japan made pottery jars during the Jomon period, which began about 10,000 B.C. They made jars of clay and hardened them by placing them in a bonfire. Later, people started firing pottery objects in pits, which were packed with burning wood. These pits acted as kilns (or ovens).

By about 5000 B.C., people of the ancient Middle East used fires to heat copper ore to a high enough temperature to release copper metal from the rocks. This process is called smelting. Copper smelting was followed by tin, lead, and silver. By 3000 B.C., metalworkers in Mesopotamia combined copper and tin to make bronze, beginning the period that historians call the Bronze Age. This was followed by smelting iron (and the Iron Age) by about 1500 B.C.

This woodcut illustration shows the process of copper smelting nearly 500 years ago. The man at the top is pouring lumps of ore into a furnace. He wears a mask as protection from the fumes.

Heating Values

Scientists work out the heating value of different substances to compare how useful and efficient they are. The value shows how much heat (in units of heat energy called megajoules) the substances produce for every kilogram burned. Here are some heating values for biomass materials:

The figures compare with coal at 15–27 megajoules and petroleum at 47.3.

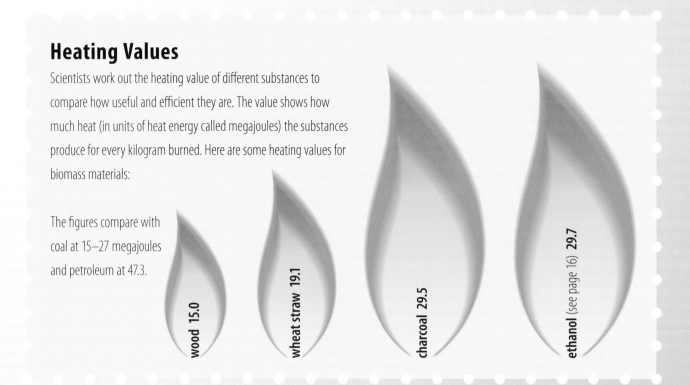

wood 15.0

wheat straw 19.1

charcoal 29.5

ethanol (see page 16) 29.7

Charcoal and Coke

Thousands of years ago, people discovered that heaping wood into piles or partly burying it before burning made it smolder slowly. This process produced charcoal, which creates more heat and gives off less smoke when it burns than wood does. During the Iron Age, charcoal was generally used in furnaces for heating iron ore to temperatures high enough to release molten iron. We still use charcoal today as fuel for barbecue grills.

Gift of the Gods

In ancient India, Hindus believed that the personification of fire, called Agni, acted as a messenger between the gods of the sky and humans on Earth. People worshipped Agni with a sacred fire. In ancient Persia, Zoroastrians believed that fire was given to humans by the great creator god, and it was worshipped as a symbol of creation and power. An ancient Persian story also tells of an epic fight between a man and a dragon. The man threw his spear at the dragon, but it missed and struck a rock. This created a spark that supposedly made fire for the first time.

This Senegalese girl has collected a container full of firewood.

Producing Steam Power

Ancient inventors realized that they could use burning wood to boil water and make steam to power machines. In the first century A.D., a Greek scientist named Hero invented a steam engine called an aeolipile. This was a hollow globe attached by pipes to a kettle. A wood fire beneath the kettle heated water to steam. Two open pipes were attached to the globe, and steam rushed out of them to turn the globe. Hero used his invention as a scientific demonstration toy and as a device to open temple doors.

The Coming of Railroads

Steam power created the new age of railroads, which started in the early nineteenth century in Britain. Most British and European locomotives had boilers fired by coal, but in the United States, wood was more plentiful and cheaper. American locomotives had tenders behind the steam engine that carried supplies of wood and water. Railroad stations had large tanks of water, so the tenders and boilers could be regularly refilled. There were large woodsheds along the track filled with regulation-sized lengths of timber, which the locomotives could pick up.

American locomotives had a smokestack (or chimney), called a bonnet or cone stack, to catch sparks from the wood fuel burned in the firebox. Between 1830 and 1865, more than 1,700 square miles (4,500 sq km) of forest were cut down to feed the "iron horses." In 1860, 90 percent of U.S. locomotives burned wood. By 1870, many had switched to coal. By then, wood was no longer as plentiful.

Central Heating

From about 200 B.C., the ancient Romans burned charcoal fires in furnaces to heat water. Hot water and air were then piped through buildings as an early form of central heating. Where there were no natural thermal pools, they used the same system to heat their famous public baths. At home, many Romans used charcoal fires in clay braziers for heating and cooking.

Fuelwood Today

India uses more than 220 million tons (200 million t) of fuelwood every year—more than any other country. More than three-quarters of the wood is used for cooking and comes from farms, small plantations, and trees and shrubs along roads and railroads rather than from forests.

Is Wood-Fired Heating Used Today?

Today, systems similar to the ancient Roman version still heat homes, run hot water systems, and power stoves. Many burn wood or some other form of solid fuel. One of the most popular forms is the wood-pellet stove, usually made of cast iron and stainless steel, that can be used indoors. There are many outdoor boilers too. Solid fuel is also burned in large furnaces to produce electricity (see page 32).

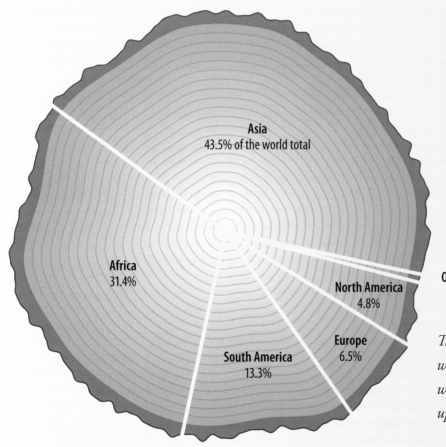

Asia
43.5% of the world total

Africa
31.4%

North America
4.8%

Oceania
0.5%

South America
13.3%

Europe
6.5%

The figures show each region's use of wood for fuel as a percentage of the world total. Asia and Africa make up three-quarters of the total.

15

Biofuels

Any biomass substance that is burned as a fuel, including wood, can be called a biofuel (which is short for biomass fuel). But today, the term is used mainly for liquid fuels that power cars and other forms of transportation. Biofuels have developed from different plants in various parts of the world, depending on what grows best in the local soil and climate.

In Europe, biofuels are mainly made from rape (a plant of the cabbage family with oil-bearing seeds), wheat, and sugar beet. In North America, corn and soybeans are common sources. In South America, sugar cane is grown for this purpose. In Southeast Asian countries, oil palms are the main source of biofuels.

Ethanol

Ethanol (or ethyl alcohol) is a type of alcohol that can be used as a biofuel. It is mass produced by fermenting plants. This means

A pump attendant in Thailand fills a car with a blend of biofuel. This is B5, which stands for 5 percent biodiesel (see page 18).

breaking down the sugar or starch in plants using microorganisms, such as those in yeast. The process is similar to brewing beer or making other alcoholic drinks, but the resulting ethanol is not suitable for drinking.

Bioethanol Fuel

Pure ethanol (known as E100, for 100 percent ethanol) can replace gasoline, which is made from oil (a fossil fuel). In Brazil, people have run their cars on bioethanol since the late 1970s, and the project promoting this has been a great success. Many Brazilian motorists use E100, and everyone has to put at least 25 percent ethanol (E25) in their fuel tank. Some cars have been specially adapted to run on biofuel, and ordinary gasoline engines can also use blends of ethanol and gasoline (called gasohol).

Biggest Ethanol Producers

The United States and Brazil produced more than four-fifths of the world's ethanol in 2007. Brazilian manufacturers use sugar cane as their source, while 98 percent of U.S. ethanol is made from corn.

The pumps show the world's top five producers of ethanol. Each figure is a percentage of the world's total production.

United States
49.6%

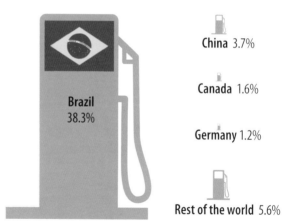

Brazil
38.3%

China 3.7%

Canada 1.6%

Germany 1.2%

Rest of the world 5.6%

Which Is Better, Cane or Corn Ethanol?

In many ways, sugar cane is a better source of biofuel than corn. From the same amount of land, cane produces nearly twice as much ethanol as corn. Cane ethanol produces eight times as much energy (which often comes from fossil fuels) as is used in its manufacture. (This is called the fuel's energy balance.)

By comparison, corn produces only one-third more output than the input energy. Cane gives off 2.4 pounds (1.1 kg) of greenhouse gases per quart (L) of fuel during production and usage. Corn fuel gives off 4.2 pounds (1.9 kg) per quart (L). Brazilian production costs for cane fuel are 20 percent lower than U.S. corn costs.

Rudolf Diesel's Fuel

In 1900, Rudolf Diesel (1858–1913), the German inventor of the diesel engine, ran one of his newly developed engines on peanut oil at the World Fair in Paris. The invention was awarded the fair's highest prize. In 1912, Diesel said, "The use of vegetable oils for engine fuels may seem insignificant today. But such oils may become in the course of time as important as the petroleum and coal tar products of the present time." Yet Diesel's engines continued to run on petroleum diesel oil (petrodiesel). It was not until the end of the twentieth century that people began taking biodiesel seriously.

Today, biodiesel is produced by extracting oil from plant seeds such as soybeans, rapeseed, or peanuts and allowing it to react with a substance such as ethanol. Small amounts can be produced with a simple press. Homemade biodiesel can be made from recycled cooking oil. Like ethanol, biodiesel can be used in its pure form (called B100) or mixed with petrodiesel. The most common blend is B20.

Different Varieties

Ethanol can be produced from a wide variety of plants. These include barley, cassava, cotton, hemp, kenaf (a form of hibiscus), corn, miscanthus (E-grass), potato, sorghum, sugar beet, sugar cane, sunflower, sweet potato, switchgrass, and wheat.

This crop of miscanthus (also called E-grass) is ready for harvesting as a form of biofuel.

Racing Around the World

In June 2008, *Earthrace*, a speedy New Zealand trimaran (three-hulled boat), set a new world record for traveling around the world in a powerboat. The feat was particularly newsworthy because *Earthrace* was powered only by biodiesel (produced mainly from soybeans and animal fats). The 79 foot (24 m) boat, with a top speed of 56 miles (90 km) per hour, took just under 61 days to circle the globe, starting and finishing on the coast of southern Spain. *Earthrace* beat the previous record by more than 13 days, despite storms and pirates.

The crew of Earthrace *waves to a welcoming crowd in Spain after powering around the world on biodiesel.*

Should Drivers Buy Eco-Cars?

New "flex" cars (flexible-fuel vehicles or FFVs) are built to run on any combination of gasohol, from 100 percent gasoline to pure ethanol. However, many older cars can also run well on lower blends of ethanol and making any new car uses a great deal of energy. Manufacturing cars also gives off greenhouse gases. From an environmental point of view, it would not be a good idea for most drivers to buy new cars, though the auto industry would approve.

Most American cars on the road today can run on gasohol blends of up to E10. Some states require up to 10 percent ethanol to be blended with gasoline. Germany is the largest consumer of bioethanol in Europe (followed by Sweden, France, and Spain) and set the level at 5 percent ethanol. The German government wanted to raise the level to 10 percent in 2008, but found that more than 3 million older German cars would have to use more expensive biofuel to work properly.

Flying on Nut Oil

Biofuels are being tested and used by all forms of transport, including commercial aircraft. In February 2008, a Virgin Atlantic jumbo jet flew from London to Amsterdam powered by a mixture of conventional petroleum-based jet fuel and biofuel. The biofuel was made from the oils of babassu nuts (from Brazilian palm trees) and coconuts. It was used to drive one of the Boeing 747's four engines.

One potential problem with biofuel is that it is more likely to freeze at very high altitudes, but this short flight was successful. Other aircraft manufacturers and airlines have also carried out test flights using biofuel. However, environmentalist groups believe this is a gimmick. They say that the aircraft and travel industries should cut the number of flights made each year to reduce greenhouse gas emissions.

Into the Second Generation

Many experts believe we are now moving into the age of second-generation biofuels. These are made from the nonfood parts of plants, such as stalks, stems, leaves, and husks, which are usually left as waste when seeds and other edible parts have been removed. Second-generation crops include nonfood plants (such as switchgrass and sunflowers) and industry waste, such as fruit skins.

Ethanol from Cell Walls

The resulting biofuel is often called cellulosic ethanol (from cellulose, which makes up the cell walls of plants). Researchers are trying to perfect the process of making ethanol from cellulose. Scientists at the U.S. Renewable Energy Laboratory have found a way to make about 306 quarts (290 L) of ethanol from 1.1 tons (1 t) of corn stalks, switchgrass, and wood. The fermentation process takes about a week.

Experts say that this process turns nearly half of the original energy content of the biomass into biofuel. They think they can increase cellulosic ethanol's energy balance (see page 17) up to 36—more than four times that of cane ethanol. The greenhouse gas emissions of the new fuel are 91 percent lower than for gasoline. But the most important thing about the second-generation fuel is that it does not compete with food (see pages 22–25).

Wood Diesel

In 2007, researchers at the University of Georgia announced that they had developed a new biofuel from wood chips and pellets. The wood is heated at high temperatures to produce charcoal, gas, and then a bio-oil. The wood diesel can be used in conventional diesel engines, and the charcoal is put back into the soil as a fertilizer.

Why Are Biofuels in the News so Much?

Biofuels are important and newsworthy for two main reasons. In the United States, the boom in biofuels stems from the government's drive to reduce the country's dependence on imported foreign oil. This is important, because America currently imports 55 percent of the oil it consumes. This figure is expected to rise to 68 percent by 2025. The government wants to use more renewable energy sources, mainly for energy security. In other parts of the world, and especially Europe, the main reason for the interest in biofuels is environmental. Governments want to reduce greenhouse gas emissions from fossil fuels.

Food versus Fuel

The main issue surrounding biomass power is the question of using plants for fuel rather than food. United Nations organizations and other research bodies highlighted the issue at conferences in 2008. International politicians, environmentalists, and others started a debate that may go on for many years.

An Unequal World

Experts have calculated that there is enough food for every person in the world to eat more than 2,700 calories of energy every day. This is more than enough for good health. But we live in an unequal world. Many people do not have enough land to grow the food they need or enough money to buy food.

Figures from the Food and Agriculture Organization (FAO) of the United Nations show that more than 852 million people do not have enough food every day to allow them to lead active, healthy lives. About 13 percent of the world's people suffer from malnutrition. The vast majority of the world's starving people (more than nine out of ten) live in developing countries. Many of them are in Africa, where more than one-third of the total population is severely malnourished.

Biogas Guzzlers

Experts have come up with many different statistics comparing the use of biomass for food and transportation. One of the most striking is that the amount of grain (maize/corn) needed to produce ethanol to fill the 24 gallon (90 L) fuel tank of a four-wheel-drive vehicle would feed one person for an entire year.

Poverty and Rising Food Prices

At a conference in 2008, FAO Director-General Jacques Diouf reported that the number of starving people in the world had increased by about 50 million in the previous year. "Poor countries are feeling the serious impact of soaring food and energy prices," he said. According to an FAO report, widespread hunger

in the world is mainly the result of poverty. Many people feel that this problem is worsened by a global rise in food prices, and these prices are partly being driven up by using plants to produce biofuels. They believe that the demand for fuel in rich countries competes with the demand for food in poor countries.

This rainforest in Malaysia was burned and cleared to make way for a palm oil plantation.

Biofuels and Deforestation

The increased demand for biofuels causes deforestation (cutting down trees and destroying forests). In Malaysia and other Southeast Asian countries, the demand for biofuels from palm oil is particularly destructive. The environmental group Friends of the Earth found that between 1985 and 2000, oil-palm plantations were responsible for severe deforestation in Malaysia. On the islands of Sumatra and Borneo, 9.9 million acres (4 million ha) of forest were cleared so the land could be used for palm farms. A further 54.4 million acres (22 million ha) are scheduled to be cleared. Environmentalists are concerned about deforestation because it adds to the effects of global warming.

BIOMASS POWER

Food Crisis

Increases in food prices have a huge impact on people in poor countries. The price of food imports goes up, while the amount of food aid from richer countries might go down. According to the FAO, food prices generally rose by nearly 40 percent in 2007 and continued to increase in 2008. The increase affected almost all crops, including corn, soybeans, palm oil, wheat, rice, and cassava. There were riots in protest in Cameroon, Egypt, Haiti, Indonesia, and Senegal. In 2008, the FAO said that 37 of the world's poorer countries were suffering from food crises, meaning that large numbers of people simply did not have enough to eat.

Creating a Dead Zone

The increase in intensive growing of corn in southern regions of Texas and Louisiana has created large dead zones in the waters of the Gulf of Mexico. The fertilizer from the farmland runs off into the Mississippi River and then into the gulf. The fertilizers in the water cause an increase in the number of algae, which reduces the oxygen in the water when they die. Fish and other marine animals then do not have enough oxygen.

This ethanol plant in the corn-growing region of Indiana produces more than 423 million quarts (400 million L) of biofuel a year.

Corn and Ethanol

How supply and demand affect food prices is illustrated by corn-produced ethanol. The increased demand for corn for biofuel encouraged farmers to grow more corn for this than for human and animal feed. As corn prices increased, consumers bought less of it and changed to wheat and rice. U.S. corn-ethanol production has more than tripled in six years.

Year	Ethanol in millions of quarts (L)		Increase
2001	7,100	(6,700)	
2002	11,200	(10,600)	58%
2005	15,618	(14,780)	39%
2006	26,000	(24,600)	66%

Pluses and Minuses

Farming crops intensively, whether for food or biofuel, has an enormous effect on the environment. Experts point out that world production of cereals, for example, increased by more than 40 percent between 1980 and 2006. But at the same time, the amount of land used to produce cereals fell by 6 percent. The increase was due to greater efficiency, but this can bring problems too. Farmers may use more fertilizer and pesticide to increase the yield of their crops. That can have an effect on the environment, even killing other plants and animals.

A Crime against Humanity?

In 2007, an important member of the United Nations' staff called the trade in biofuels "a crime against humanity." He admitted that there were strong arguments for biofuels in terms of energy efficiency and combating the greenhouse effect and global warming. But he believed that the effects on the world's starving people outweighed these arguments, and he called for a five-year ban on biofuel production.

Many people agreed when they learned that in Swaziland, in southern Africa, the government was exporting biofuel made from cassava, one of the country's staple crops. It decided to do this despite the fact that 40 percent of Swaziland's people were facing severe food shortages in the drought-stricken country. The environmental campaigner George Monbiot said simply: "It doesn't get madder than this."

Powerful Waste

Biomass power can also be developed from organic waste matter. Scientists are looking for new ways to do this because using waste has enormous benefits for the environment. Most people agree that using rotting material from waste dumps and landfill sites is a good idea. There are costs involved in collecting bioenergy and turning it into useful power, but the raw materials are plentiful and free.

Biogas

Natural gas—the fossil fuel we find underground near oil deposits —is made mainly of methane. This gas forms when organic materials, such as dead plants, decay in places where there is no oxygen. Bacteria and other microbes break the material down, releasing methane and carbon dioxide. This happens naturally at the bottom of ponds and swamps. The resulting methane is often called marsh gas. A similar process happens in landfill sites, where waste is dumped in a large hole in the ground. The waste is covered by further deposits—as happens naturally in a marsh—and these keep air and oxygen away from the lower layers of waste. The biogas builds up, comes to the surface, and rises into the atmosphere if it is not captured and collected.

Waste Food

In many rich countries, most people throw away vast quantities of food. Much of this is leftover food, but some is edible food that people do not want or that they have stored too long. A great deal of this organic matter ends up in landfill sites. International leaders have acknowledged this at economic conferences and are encouraging people to waste less food. The process of biogas collection means that this waste can be put to a useful purpose.

The Process

The process of biogas production is called anaerobic digestion, which means breaking down substances without oxygen. The waste material is usually fed into a large metal tank called a digester. The biogas rises to the top of the digester where it can be siphoned off through a pipe. The remainder of the waste sinks to the bottom of the digester as a semiliquid mass, or slurry, that can sometimes be used on farmland as a fertilizer to enrich the soil.

This digester in Germany is used to produce fertilizer as well as biogas.

Could We Burn Biogas Instead of Natural Gas?

Yes, we could. Experts calculate that 35 cubic feet (1 cu m) of biogas can produce enough power to cook three meals for a family of six. However, there are problems. The natural gas piped to our homes is very clean. To make usable biogas, various amounts of water, carbon dioxide, hydrogen sulfide (a gas that smells like rotten eggs), and other particles would have to be removed. This is an expensive process, so it is generally better to use biogas in other ways.

Running on Waste Beer

A company in Sweden makes biogas from bottles and cans of beer, wine, and spirits that have been seized by Swedish customs authorities. They make nearly 423,000 quarts (400,000 L) of alcohol a year from alcohol that customs used to pour away. The liquids are mixed with other waste, such as inedible meat products from slaughterhouses. The mixture is heated to 158°F (70°C), put into a digester, and left to rot for 30 days. The biogas this produces powers trucks, buses, cars, and a train. The Swedish biogas train's greenhouse gas emissions are much lower than those of the diesel engine that the biogas has replaced as shown by the following figures.

The Swedish biogas train has a top speed of 80 miles (130 km) per hour and can travel for 370 miles (600 km) before needing to refill with gas.

	old diesel engine	new biogas engine
nitrogen oxide	6.15	2.00
non-methane hydrocarbons	0.35	0.10
carbon monoxide	0.60	0.01
particles	0.16	0.01

All the emission figures are in grams per kilowatt-hour (g/kWh). This is a unit of energy equal to the work done by one kilowatt (see opposite) in one hour.

Gobar Gas

Gobar is the Hindi word for cow dung. There are many gobar gas plants in India and Pakistan. A gobar digester plant has a round concrete pit built near cattle sheds. Cow dung goes directly to the pit where waste water is added. The dung breaks down, giving off biogas, which is piped to individual homes nearby. The slurry left in the digester is used as a fertilizer. Gobar gas has replaced firewood for cooking in many rural areas of southern India.

Converting to Gas

Another use for biomass waste is to convert it into a gas by a process called gasification. Waste materials such as rice husks and coconut shells are heated to very high temperatures with little oxygen in devices called reactors. The biomass gives off a mixture of gases, including hydrogen and carbon monoxide. This mixture is called a syngas (or synthetic gas) and can be further treated with heat and pressure to produce methane.

From Wood to Gas

Wood chips and sawdust can be converted in a wood gas generator (also called a gasifier). The wood waste is heated to a temperature greater than 1290°F (700°C) and gives off gases. The first wood gas generator was built by the German scientist Gustav Bischof in 1839. By 1901, early cars were running on wood gas. The development of cheaper and more efficient fuels meant that scientists have returned to the use of wood gas only in recent years.

What Is a Watt?

A watt (W) is a unit of power that measures the rate of producing or using energy. The term was named after Scottish engineer James Watt (1736–1819), who developed an improved steam engine. Watt measured his engine's performance in horsepower (hp). One horsepower equals 746 watts. Today, watts are generally used to measure electric power.

1 kilowatt (kW) = 1 thousand watts
1 megawatt (MW) = 1 million watts
1 gigawatt (GW) = 1 billion watts

Encouraging People to Go Green

Countries are looking for new ways to encourage people to use biofuels, biogas, and other environmentally friendly fuels. One way is to subsidize production to keep the price of renewable energy fuels down. In Sweden, the government encourages green drivers by allowing them to park free in many cities and not to pay road tolls. In 2007, as many as 40,000 Swedish cars used environmentally friendly fuels, but that is just 1 percent of the total. The percentage is much higher among new cars—20 percent of these run on some form of biofuel.

Generating Electricity

Biomass can generate electricity in a variety of ways. The traditional method involves burning plant material, especially wood, to produce heat. This is then used to boil water and create steam. A report, by experts at Imperial College, London, predicted that biomass could produce nearly one-quarter of the world's electricity by 2020.

Turbines and Generators

Inside a bioelectricity power plant, electrical power is produced by a generator. In 1831, British scientist Michael Faraday (1791–1867) discovered he could create electricity by moving a magnet through a coil of copper wire. This process, called electromagnetic induction, led to the invention of the electric generator, which works by changing mechanical energy into electrical energy. In biomass-fired power plants, steam provides the mechanical energy by turning the rotor blades of a turbine. The blades are connected to a shaft, which is also attached to a generator.

World's Leading Producers

The United States produces nearly one-third of the world's bioelectricity. This is much more than any other country. This chart depicts the leading countries in 2005.

USA 30.7%
Germany 7.3%
Brazil 7.3%
Japan 5.1%
Finland 4.9%
UK 4.7%
Canada 4.6%
Spain 4.3%
Rest of the world 31.1%

Altering the Balance of Nature

One of the environmental problems caused by bioelectricity production is that biomass crops involve growing large amounts of one type of plant in the same place. This might be fast-growing willow trees or miscanthus grass. It can lead to an increase in pests so that more pesticides are needed to control them. These can damage the soil and surrounding environment. One way to avoid this is to use waste biomass, such as material from sawmills.

This enormous pile of wood chips fuels Japan's largest biomass power station. The plant burns more than 220,000 tons (200,000 t) of wood chips a year.

Inside the generator, the shaft makes magnets spin inside wire coils to produce electricity.

Sources of Biomass

The main source for electricity production is solid biomass—wood and other plant material, especially bagasse (see page 33). This makes up nearly three-quarters of electricity production. Other sources are biogas (produced by gasification, see page 29), liquid biomass such as vegetable oils, and material from landfill and other waste sites. All four sources have increased production recently, and there has been an overall increase of 75 percent in 10 years.

Biogas Plants

Another way of using biomass to generate electricity is to turn the organic matter into biogas (see page 26). This then can be used to turn the blades of a gas turbine rather than a steam turbine. Some biogas power plants are fired by sawdust, which burns in a furnace to produce the gas to drive the turbine. The hot gas can even be used a second time, heating water to turn a separate steam turbine and generate more electricity.

Electricity Production from Biomass

	1995	2005
Solid biomass	85.3	134.9
Biogas	6.0	24.8
Municipal waste	13.4	22.8
Liquid biomass	0.0	0.9
Total	104.7	183.4

Figures are in terawatt-hours (TWh). A terawatt is 1 trillion watts (see page 29).

BIOMASS POWER

Steven's Croft power plant in Scotland uses more than 530,000 tons (480,000 t) of biomass fuel a year.

Sawdust and Wood

In 2008, a new bioelectric plant opened in Scotland that produces a total of 44 megawatts (MW). It is powerful enough to generate electricity for 70,000 homes. When it opened, the Steven's Croft plant was powered mainly by sawdust and waste products, such as small round wood from local sawmills. In the future, the plant will burn fast-growing willow trees that are being grown for the purpose by local farmers. This will help provide local jobs.

Around the World

Sugar cane and bagasse are available in many countries around the world, as shown in this chart of the top 10 bagasse producers.

Production in millions of tons (t)

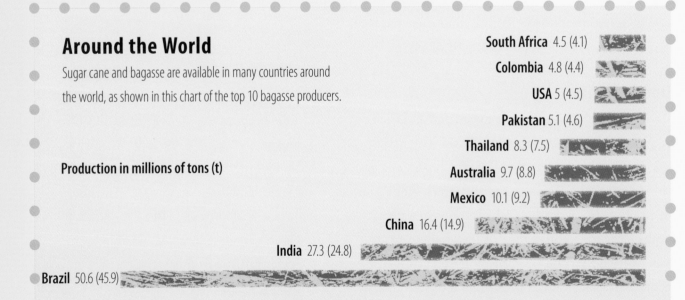

South Africa 4.5 (4.1)
Colombia 4.8 (4.4)
USA 5 (4.5)
Pakistan 5.1 (4.6)
Thailand 8.3 (7.5)
Australia 9.7 (8.8)
Mexico 10.1 (9.2)
China 16.4 (14.9)
India 27.3 (24.8)
Brazil 50.6 (45.9)

Bagasse

Bagasse (from a Spanish word for pulp) is the name of the mushy substance left over when sugar-cane stalks have been crushed to remove their juice. About 1.1 tons (1 t) of raw sugar cane provides about 330 pounds (150 kg) of sugar and leaves about 200 pounds (90 kg) of bagasse. This waste material makes excellent biomass fuel and is often burned to power sugar mills. This usually leaves enough bagasse for purposes such as generating electricity. As the technology is the same as for coal-powered plants, biomass is sometimes combined with coal. The furnaces can use either fuel. In some places, bagasse is used for part of the year (when it is available) and coal the rest of the time.

Changing Technology

A power station in Lahti, north of the Finnish capital of Helsinki, started producing electricity from oil-fired boilers in 1976. Six years later, the plant changed to coal. In 1998, it added bark, wood chips, and sawdust to the fuel mix. Today, it also recycles and gasifies household and industrial waste. This is a good example of combining and changing technology to suit the times.

Combined Heat and Power

Biomass is increasingly used to power combined heat and power (CHP) plants. The plants are based on a system called cogeneration —the production of two types of energy. The plants achieve this by first producing bioelectricity. The extra or waste heat in the form of steam from the turbines then is used to heat nearby homes, factories, and other buildings.

Is There Enough Biomass?

Biomass is constantly produced all over the world. Climate affects the kind of biomass that thrives in any particular region. Sugar cane, for example, grows well in warm regions, while willow and similar plants provide useful biomass in cooler climates. In Australia, fast-growing eucalyptus bushes and trees add to the fuel mix. Overall, experts calculate that just one-eighth of the biomass grown every year in the world would be enough to provide us with fuel for all the energy we need. However, there are problems, such as the effect on agriculture and land use. There is also the big question of whether we should concentrate on growing fuel or food (see pages 22–25).

33

A Good Source of Hydrogen

Biomass can be used to produce the gas hydrogen (see page 29 on the gasification process). Hydrogen is the simplest and most abundant element in the universe. It combines with carbon to form petroleum and other hydrocarbons and fossil fuels. It also combines with oxygen to form water (the word hydrogen means producing water).

Hydrogen is not an energy source, because we always need energy to produce it, but it is useful as a carrier of energy. Most importantly, it can be used as a fuel to generate electricity, and biomass can play a part in this. Biomass-produced hydrogen can be collected by a special process. It can then be burned to produce heat or, even better, fed into a fuel cell to generate electricity.

Fuel Cells

Just like electric generators, fuel cells convert chemical energy to electrical energy. One of the most useful type of fuel cell generates electricity by combining hydrogen (H) and oxygen (O), which then form water (H_2O). As the electricity is produced, water is given off as a harmless waste product. This is one of the reasons why environmentalists are very keen on this technology.

A fuel cell will produce electricity as long as it is supplied with the two gases. Air is easily available

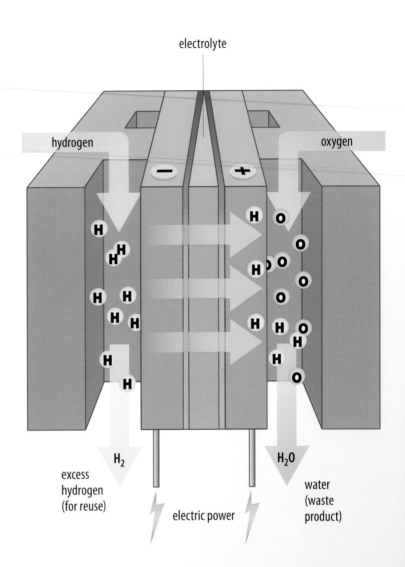

A hydrogen fuel cell. Hydrogen passes through negative (-) and positive (+) electrodes. The electrolyte is a chemical compound that can conduct electricity.

New Research

In 2007, Japanese research scientists reported that they were working on a new kind of fuel cell. It is powered by glucose, a simple sugar that plants produce by photosynthesis (see page 7). The glucose comes from organic matter by a fermentation process that is similar to the natural process of plants.

Could Fuel Cells Power Cars?

Car manufacturers are developing cars especially for fuel cell technology, but there are still problems. The technology is expensive, hydrogen is not easy to store, and the cells can be slow to warm up, which means that engine performance is not always good. Nevertheless, many experts believe that these will be the cars of the future. In the United States, the Department of Energy runs a Hydrogen, Fuel Cells & Infrastructure Technologies Program, which states: "Fuel cells are an important enabling technology for the hydrogen economy and have the potential to revolutionize the way we power our nation, offering cleaner, more efficient alternatives to the combustion of gasoline and other fossil fuels. Fuel cells have the potential to replace the internal combustion engine in vehicles and provide power in stationary and portable power applications because they are energy-efficient, clean, and fuel-flexible. Hydrogen or any hydrogen-rich fuel can be used by this emerging technology."

as the source of oxygen, but hydrogen is not so easy to supply. This is where biomass gasification comes in. It is a far better method, for example, than splitting off hydrogen from water. This can be done, but the process involves using a great deal of energy. Another source of hydrogen is hydrocarbons, but they give off a lot of carbon dioxide during the process, which increases the greenhouse effect.

The Ford Airstream concept car was first shown at a car show in Detroit, Michigan, in 2007. The car is driven by an electric motor powered by batteries that are charged by a hydrogen fuel cell system. The car's exhaust gives off water vapor.

What Does the Future Hold?

Experts agree that the world's demand for energy will increase sharply over the next few decades. The International Energy Agency says that the world's energy needs will be more than 50 percent higher in 2030 than in 2007.

Much of the increased demand will be from developing countries as they try to enjoy the same advantages as the world's richer nations. During the same period, the demand for electricity will double. This means that renewable energy sources, such as biomass, will become even more important.

A New Vision?

Many developments in energy use have come from discoveries and inventions by inspired individuals. One example is Rudolf Diesel, who designed and built his own car engine and ran it

Fuel of the Future

In 1925, Henry Ford thought the future lay with biofuels. He said, "The fuel of the future is going to come from fruit . . . from apples, weeds, sawdust, almost anything. There is fuel in every bit of vegetable matter that can be fermented . . . There's enough alcohol in one year's yield of an acre of potatoes to drive the machinery necessary to cultivate the fields for one hundred years." The discovery of vast amounts of oil, in the Middle East and elsewhere, changed people's views for the rest of the twentieth century. Perhaps now biomass really could be the fuel of the future.

Research scientists constantly make new discoveries about biomass.

The surface of this pond is covered with algae. These plantlike organisms could form a fuel of the future.

on peanut oil (see page 18). Another great pioneer, Henry Ford (1863–1947), is most famous for his development of the mass production of cars, especially his Tin Lizzie cars—the Model-T Ford. But Ford also recognized the value and importance of biofuels and ran early cars on ethanol made from hemp (a tough, woody plant). Perhaps new advances will come in the twenty-first century from scientists, researchers, engineers, or industrialists who have a similar vision and will develop biomass systems that we are unaware of today.

Third-Generation Biofuels

Experts believe that we will increasingly use second-generation biofuels (see page 20). Many also think that a third generation is just around the corner. This future generation of biofuels will be based on algae. These simple organisms are similar to plants and live mainly in water. The best known examples of algae are different kinds of seaweed. These include pond scum, such as what you find if you leave a bucket of water outside for a few weeks. Researchers all over the world are working on processes to produce biofuel from algae collected from ponds, lakes, rivers, and even sewage farms. They say it is possible to produce more than 105,700 quarts (100,000 L) of ethanol a year from 2.5 acres (1 ha) of algae. This is 13 times more productive than sugar cane. It is possible that people could produce their own fuel at home using algae collected from the roofs of their homes.

Moving to Nonfood Biomass

The U.S. Office of Biomass program predicts that in the future biofuels will come from different sources. Today's sources include:

• grains (corn/maize, sorghum, wheat);

• oilseeds and plants (soybeans).

Future sources include:

• agricultural residues (stalks, stems, other crop wastes);

• energy crops (switchgrass, miscanthus, poplar, willow);

• forest sources (wood waste, forest thinnings, small-diameter trees);

• oilseeds and oil crops (algae, jatropha—a succulent plant);

• green wastes (urban wood wastes, sorted municipal solid waste).

Sewage-Fuel

A company in New Zealand claims to be the first to produce affordable biofuel from wild algae harvested from open-air environments. The company gets algae from the settling ponds of a local sewage farm. The New Zealand minister for energy has tested a car powered by the company's new biofuel. The company also has a joint project with an aircraft company to develop algae jet fuel.

Funding Research

In the future, governments and energy companies will need to put more and more money into researching and developing renewable energy sources—including biomass. In 2007, the global energy giant BP

The Santa Elisa ethanol plant, in Brazil, continues to expand and produce more biofuel.

Workers pick through rubbish in a landfill in southwestern China. Landfills could provide more biofuels in the future.

announced that it was setting up a research organization called the Energy Biosciences Institute. BP's partners in the institute are two universities (California and Illinois) and a scientific laboratory (Lawrence Berkeley National Laboratory). The energy company is putting $500 million into its research program, which will explore "how bioscience [the study of living organisms] can be used to increase energy production and reduce the impact of energy consumption on the environment." The institute's first projects will focus on renewable biofuels for road transportation.

Using More Biofuels

According to the latest estimates by the U.S. Department of Energy, America is likely to use much more cellulosic biofuel (see page 21) in the future:

2,000 million quarts (1,900 million L) by 2012
12,150 million quarts (11,500 million L) by 2015
64,460 million quarts (61,000 million L) by 2022

Are Any Scientists Against Biomass Power?

Some are because of the problems of deforestation or the food versus fuel issue. James Lovelock is an influential scientist and environmentalist. He developed the theory of Gaia—planet Earth seen as a living organism.

In 2006, he wrote: "Used sensibly and on a modest scale, burning wood or agricultural waste for heat or energy is no threat to Gaia [Earth organism], but we have to remind ourselves that biofuel, when harvested in a large-scale operation, is a menace. It is only renewable if it has no effect on the natural cycle of carbon. Biofuels are especially dangerous because it is too easy to grow them as a replacement for fossil fuel; they will then demand an area of land or ocean far larger than Gaia can afford . . . We have already taken more than half of the productive land to grow food for ourselves. How can we expect Gaia to manage the Earth if we try to take the rest of the land for fuel production?"

Changing Biomass Genes

All plants (and animals) have biological sets of instructions within their cells. These coded instructions are carried by genes, which pass the code on to the next generation. In recent years, scientists have learned how to alter an organism's genes. This is called genetic modification. Genetically modified (GM) foods are already on sale in our supermarkets.

Genes are made of a substance called DNA (deoxyribonucleic acid). When the DNA of a plant or an animal is altered by humans, it is known as a genetically modified organism (GMO). Genetic modification can change the characteristics of an organism, such as its resistance to certain chemicals or its rate of growth. The biggest GM producing countries are the United States, Argentina, Canada, China, Brazil, and South Africa.

This crop of genetically modified corn is growing in a field in England. It could be used for biofuel.

GM Research

One of the Energy Biosciences Institute's early projects focuses on the genetic improvement of bioenergy crops. It looks specifically at improving the characteristics of giant miscanthus grass.

Popular GM crops are soybeans, corn, cotton, and oilseed rape. All these can be used for producing biofuel, so scientists will be looking at using GM to improve them.

Using Plant Cells

Lignin is a substance formed by plant cells that helps to make plants strong and stiff. It is similar to cellulose (see page 21) and often burned to generate steam and run the biofuel process. Scientists are looking at ways to genetically alter the lignin content of certain plants so they would be even more useful. Others are trying to find ways to make lignin in a laboratory. The science of biomass may change dramatically in the coming years.

Climate Change

In the future, people's attitudes toward biomass power and all other forms of renewable energy will depend on global warming and general climate change. Since 2000, there has been a great deal of interest in this topic. Forecasts by the Intergovernmental Panel on Climate Change (IPCC) and other research organizations cause concern. An IPCC report in 2007 stated that most of the increase in world temperatures since the mid-twentieth century was due to the emission of greenhouse gases by human activity. This means that burning carbon-neutral biomass materials instead of fossil fuels will help to combat climate change. The International Energy Agency says, "Urgent action is needed if greenhouse-gas concentrations are to be stabilized at a level that would prevent dangerous interference with the climate system."

More Environmental Concerns

Many environmentalists are against GM. They say that GM crops are unnatural, man-made organisms that may turn out to be dangerous to both the environment and human health. They believe that GM crops could spread to non-GM plants, wipe out natural species, and reduce biodiversity (the world's wide range of plants and animals). This could also leave farmers in the hands of giant companies that control GM seeds that may carry health risks that we will only find out about when it is too late.

Combined Production

Many experts believe that CHP technology (combined heat and power, see page 33) will become more useful in the future. It makes sense to use power for two purposes when possible. It also makes sense to combine energy sources as some power stations do today by running biomass plants alongside coal-fired furnaces and turbines. Perhaps scientists will find new ways to combine biomass with other renewable sources of energy, such as wind, water, and solar power.

Large and Small Power Stations

Biomass will continue to be an important energy source for large power stations, especially in the industrialized world. In poorer countries, biomass will work well for smaller local stations. In northwest India, for example, more than 200 biogas digesters (see page 27) have been installed around Ranthambhore National Park, which is famous for its protected tigers. Cow dung produces gas for cooking, which reduces the need to gather wood and helps to protect the natural life of an important wildlife reserve.

Pipes and tanks at a biodiesel plant in Brazil. The country currently produces much more ethanol, but biodiesel production is likely to grow in the next few years.

What about Cost?

People are concerned about the cost of energy, including electricity at home and fuel costs for their car. The price of biomass energy varies according to the source. It can be changed and lowered with help from governments. In some countries, biomass and other renewable sources are helped by a feed-in tariff to compete with fossil fuels. This is the price per unit of electricity that a national or regional energy supplier pays for renewable electricity from private generators.

The government regulates the tariff (or price). In Germany, for example, this is covered by a Renewable Energy Law, which is updated regularly. As biomass technology improves, its costs and prices will come down. The U.S. Department of Energy forecasts that the selling price of cellulosic ethanol (see page 21) will decrease. It sold at nearly $6 dollars per gallon ($1.60 per L) in 2001, fell to $2.20 per gallon ($0.58 per L) in 2007, and should fall to about $1 per gallon ($0.26 per L) by 2012.

Settling the Food Dilemma

Increased use of biomass for energy will depend on settling the food versus fuel dilemma (see pages 22–25), which depends on tackling the problems of world poverty and starvation. As long as these problems exist, some people will view crops as a source of food that is threatened by their use as fuel. Scientists who take a long-term view might concentrate more on combating the problems of climate change. Others may be more concerned with the plight of the world's poor people.

Creating Jobs

Experts have calculated that producing biofuels creates many more jobs than other energy sources. This is particularly useful in developing countries, where jobs are scarce. This chart shows the jobs created in numbers of workers per year for the same amount of energy produced (1 TWh).

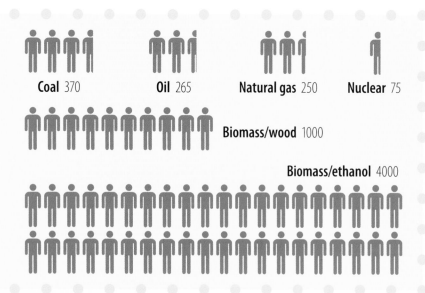

Coal 370   **Oil** 265   **Natural gas** 250   **Nuclear** 75

Biomass/wood 1000

Biomass/ethanol 4000

Glossary

algae   A group of simple plantlike organisms that includes seaweed.

anaerobic digestion   Breaking things down in the absence of oxygen.

bacteria   Single-celled microorganisms that often cause decay.

bagasse   A pulpy mass left after juice has been removed from sugar cane.

biodiversity   A wide variety of living things.

biofuel   A fuel produced from biomass, such as ethanol from sugar cane.

biogas   Gas fuel produced by biomass, especially methane.

carbon cycle   A series of linked processes in which carbon is exchanged between living things and the nonliving world.

carbon dioxide (CO_2)   A greenhouse gas given off when fossil fuels burn.

carbon monoxide   A poisonous gas given off when fossil fuels burn without enough air.

cellulose   A substance that makes up the cell walls of plants.

charcoal   A black form of carbon made by heating wood.

consumer   An organism that feeds on other organisms (such as an animal on plants).

decomposer   An organism (such as a bacterium) that causes organic matter to decay.

deforestation   Cutting down trees and removing woods and forests.

digester   A tank in which biomass decomposes and produces biogas.

DNA (deoxyribonucleic acid)   A substance in living things that carries genetic information.

ecosystem   A group of living things that are dependent on each other and their environment.

electromagnetic radiation   The range of electrical and magnetic radiation given off by the Sun; includes radio waves and visible light.

energy security   The knowledge (or an attempt to make sure) that there will always be enough energy available.

ethanol (ethyl alcohol)   A liquid biofuel that can be produced from plants such as sugar cane and corn.

fossil fuel   A fuel (such as coal, oil, or natural gas) that comes from the remains of prehistoric plants and animals.

gene   The basic unit of DNA that passes characteristics from one generation of living things to the next.

generator   A machine that turns mechanical energy into electrical energy.

global warming   Heating up of Earth's surface, especially caused by pollution from burning fossil fuels.

GM (genetic modification)   Changing the makeup of genes in living things so that they have particular characteristics (such as a resistance to disease).

greenhouse effect   Warming of Earth's surface caused especially by pollution from burning fossil fuels.

hydrocarbon   A chemical compound containing hydrogen and carbon.

hydrogen   A light, colorless gas that combines with oxygen to make water.

lignin   A substance in the cell walls of plants.

megajoule   One million joules (a joule is a unit of energy).

methane   A flammable gas that forms when organic matter decays; it is the main element of natural gas.

microbe   A microscopic organism.

nonrenewable energy or resource   Energy or a resource that is used up and cannot be replaced (from sources such as coal, gas, oil, or uranium).

oxygen   A colorless gas that humans and animals need to breathe to live.

pesticide   A chemical substance used to kill pests such as insects.

photosynthesis   The process that plants use to make their own food from carbon dioxide and water.

producer   An organism (such as a plant) that produces its own food.

renewable energy or resource   Energy or a resource that does not run out by being used (such as biomass, geothermal, solar, water, and wind power).

Web Sites

A BBC Quick Guide to Biofuels

http://news.bbc.co.uk/1/hi/sci/tech/6294133.stm

Biomass Energy Basics from the U.S. National Renewable Energy Laboratory

www.nrel.gov/learning/re_biomass.html

World Maps from the Global Energy Network Institute on Bioenergy Sources

www.geni.org/globalenergy/library/renewable-energy-resources/bioenergy.shtml

Ethanol Myths and Facts from the U.S. Deparment of Energy

www1.eere.energy.gov/biomass/ethanol_myths_facts.html

Index